The Oklahoma City National Memorial

CORNERSTONES OF FREEDOM

SECOND SERIES

R. Conrad Stein

Children's Press®
A Division of Scholastic Inc.
New York • Toronto • London • Auckland • Sydney
Mexico City • New Delhi • Hong Kong
Danbury, Connecticut

Photographs © 2003: AP/Wide World Photos: 17 (Lacy Atkins), 6, 32, 45 top left, 27 bottom (J. Pat Carter), 18 (Dale Fulkerson), 12, 24 top (Stephen Holman), 33 (Jerry Laizure), 7, 22 bottom, 23, 45 bottom right (David Longstreath), 19 (Noble County Jail), 8, 10, 25 (David J. Phillip), cover top (Laura Rauch), 11 (Rick Bowmer), 24 bottom (Amy Sancetta), 13 (Greg Smith), 4, 5, 22 top, 44 left; Corbis Images: 34, 45 top right (AFP), 41 (Paul Buck/AFP), 27 top (Richard Hamilton Smith), 26 (Maps.com), 31, 35 top (Reuters NewMedia Inc.), 9 (Bob Rowan/Progressive Image), 20 (Mike Segar/Reuters NewMedia Inc.); Corbis Sygma: 35 bottom (Mark Kraus), 37 (Jesus Rodriguez); Getty Images: cover bottom (J. Pat Carter/Newsmakers), 21 bottom (Dallas Morning News/Liaison), 16 (Kok Family), 3, 30, 38 (David McNeese/Newsmakers), 28, 29, 45 bottom left (Jeff Mitchell/Reuters), 21 top (Reuters), 36 (Greg Ruggiero), 14, 15, 44 right (Hugh Scott/Liaison).

Library of Congress Cataloging-in-Publication Data

Stein, R. Conrad.
   The Oklahoma City National Memorial / R. Conrad Stein.
       p. cm. — (Cornerstones of freedom. Second series)
   Summary: Describes the events surrounding the 1995 bombing of the
Murrah Federal Building in Oklahoma City and the memorial created to
honor the victims.
   Includes bibliographical references and index.
      ISBN 0-516-24205-9
      1. Oklahoma City Federal Building Bombing, Oklahoma City, Okla.,
1995—Juvenile literature. 2. Bombings—Oklahoma—Oklahoma
City—Juvenile literature. 3. Terrorism—Oklahoma—Oklahoma City—
Juvenile literature. 4. Memorials—Oklahoma—Oklahoma City—Juvenile
literature. 5. Oklahoma City National Memorial (Okla.) [1. Oklahoma City
Federal Building Bombing, Oklahoma City, Okla., 1995. 2. Oklahoma
City National Memorial (Okla.)] I. Title. II. Series.
HV6432 .S736 2003
976.6'38053—dc21
                                                      2002012653

CHILDREN'S PRESS, AND CORNERSTONES OF FREEDOM™, and
associated logos are trademarks and or registered trademarks of Grolier
Publishing Co., Inc. SCHOLASTIC and associated logos are trademarks
and or registered trademarks of Scholastic Inc.

1 2 3 4 5 6 7 8 9 10 R 12 11 10 09 08 07 06 05 04 03

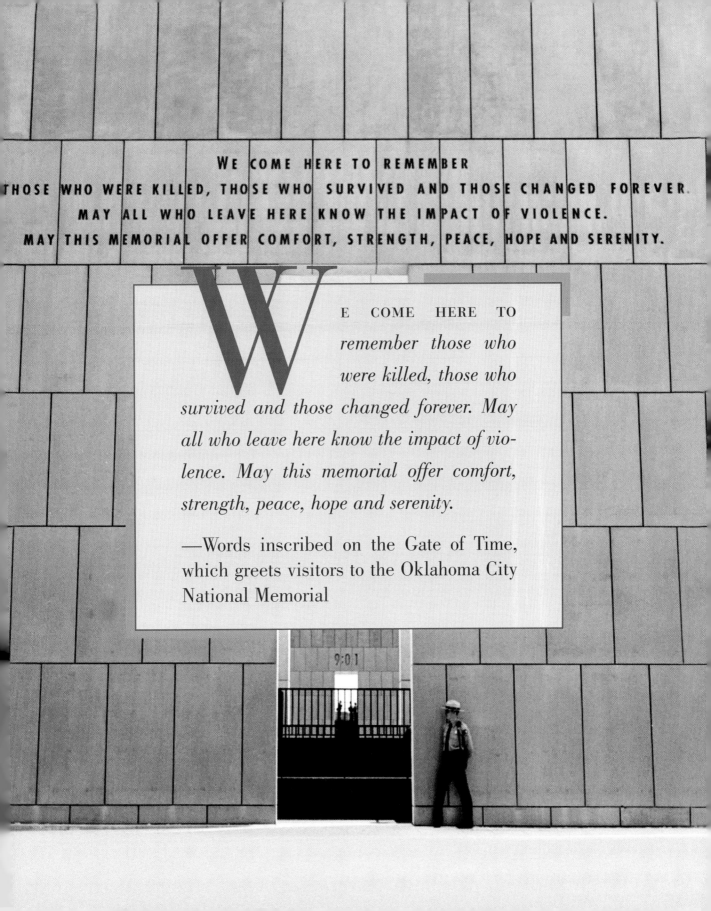

WE COME HERE TO REMEMBER
THOSE WHO WERE KILLED, THOSE WHO SURVIVED AND THOSE CHANGED FOREVER.
MAY ALL WHO LEAVE HERE KNOW THE IMPACT OF VIOLENCE.
MAY THIS MEMORIAL OFFER COMFORT, STRENGTH, PEACE, HOPE AND SERENITY.

WE COME HERE TO remember those who were killed, those who survived and those changed forever. May all who leave here know the impact of violence. May this memorial offer comfort, strength, peace, hope and serenity.

—Words inscribed on the Gate of Time, which greets visitors to the Oklahoma City National Memorial

The Murrah building seen before the April 19, 1995, terrorist bombing.

A DAY LIKE ANY OTHER

April 19, 1995, dawned sunny and warm in Oklahoma City, Oklahoma. It was spring, and birds sang from the downtown trees. Government employees at the Alfred P. Murrah Federal Office Building were at their desks by 9:00 A.M. The nine-story building housed seventeen federal government agencies and served as a workplace for more than five hundred men and women. People were constantly coming and going from Murrah offices. Senior citizens applied for Social Security on one floor. On another floor young men and women spoke with recruiters from the U.S. Army and the Marine Corps.

Parents loved the day-care center, which occupied most of the second floor. Called America's Kids, the center had separate rooms for babies and toddlers. Bright colors created a happy atmosphere. Drawings and cutouts by the children decorated the walls and windows. Moms and dads who worked downtown dropped their children off at the center in the morning, visited them at lunchtime, and then picked them up at the end of the day.

Shortly before nine that morning, a man parked a yellow rental truck from the Ryder Company in front of the Murrah building. The driver, a thin young man, got out and slammed the truck door behind him. He casually walked down the street. After walking about a block, the man broke into a

Alfred P. Murrah

THE NAMESAKE

Completed in 1977, Oklahoma City's federal building was named after Judge Alfred P. Murrah (1904–1975). Orphaned as a young boy, Murrah grabbed rides on freight trains to relieve his loneliness. When he was thirteen, a railroad guard kicked him off a train in a railyard in Oklahoma City. Murrah got a job there and went back to school. Eventually, at age thirty-two, he became the youngest man in history to be appointed a U.S. district court judge.

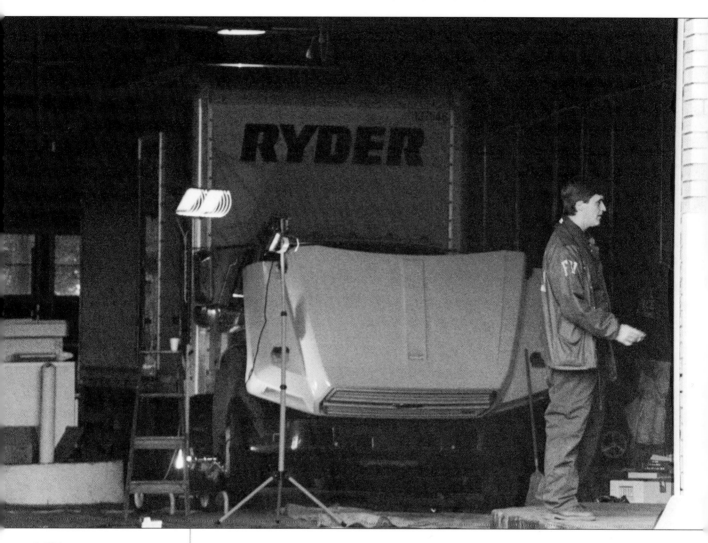

A FBI agent uses an undamaged Ryder truck to determine how the bomb was planted.

trot. He wore a T-shirt with an odd image and a message on the back. Drawn on the shirt was a picture of a tree that had blood dripping from its branches. Under the tree was a quotation from Thomas Jefferson, the third president of the United States: "THE TREE OF LIBERTY MUST BE REFRESHED FROM TIME TO TIME WITH THE BLOOD OF PATRIOTS AND TYRANTS."

At 9:02 A.M. calamity came to Oklahoma City.

In one blinding second, a ball of orange fire enveloped the federal building. An explosion roared with such deafening power it was heard 30 miles (48 kilometers) away. Pedestrians near the blast were lifted from their feet and thrown to the ground. A thick blanket of smoke covered the scene, turning the bright day into an eerie midnight. For a full five minutes bricks, plaster, and **shards** of glass rained from the sky.

Injured bomb victims line the sidewalks and streets outside the Murrah building.

Rhonda Griffin, who worked for the U.S. government, was typing at her computer on the seventh floor when the explosion ripped through the building. She remembered, "I heard something go SWOOOOOOOOSH, and everything went gray. I thought my computer had blown up . . . I started feeling things hitting me, and I thought, 'Oh my God, the computer has blown the ceiling down.' Things kept hitting [me], and I began to think that maybe I had fallen asleep at my desk and was having a bad nightmare. Then again, maybe I had lost my mind!"

Florence Rogers, a supervisor in the Federal Employees Credit Union office, said, "It felt like a whirling tornado hit, turning and twisting me and the chair. I never heard the explosion, although there was a lot of noise like an Oklahoma windstorm . . . I was sucked out of the chair and

Medical assistants Janet Froehlich, left, Wilma Jackson, middle, and Kerri Albright, right, run from the Murrah Federal Building after being told another bomb device had been found.

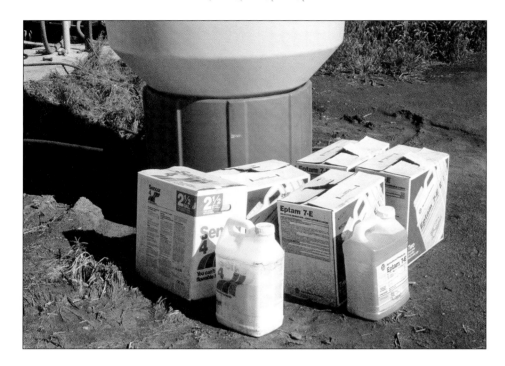

Liquid fertilizer, which is commonly used by farmers, was a key ingredient in the homemade bomb.

THE TRUCK BOMB

The tremendous blast was caused by a homemade bomb inside the Ryder truck parked on the north side of the Murrah building. Investigators later determined the truck bomb weighed 4,800 pounds (2,177 kilograms) and was made primarily from farm fertilizer and fuel oil. It was ignited with a fuse lit by the driver. The explosion caused the front of the nine-story building to rise up and then collapse—all in a few seconds.

slammed against the floor . . . A steel beam lay right beside me, and piles of debris were everywhere. I could see blue sky instead of walls and ceilings."

Police and fire units arrived in minutes. One fireman radioed his headquarters. In a shocked voice, as if he could not believe the scene that appeared before him, he said, "This is [unit] six hundred. The whole front of the federal building is gone—all floors to the roof."

The young man who had parked the rental truck in front of the Murrah building was only two blocks away when the tremendous blast **resounded** behind him. He apparently did not look back. Only he knew what thoughts raced through his mind. The man entered a parking lot and unlocked a rusty looking automobile. He had placed the car in the lot the day before, as a getaway vehicle. At first

★ ★ ★ ★

Workers rushed to the scene after the blast and attempted to rescue people trapped on the upper floors.

the car would not start. He tried again and again, and finally the engine rumbled to life. With tires screeching, the car sped away from the smoke and the horror enveloping downtown Oklahoma City.

April 19, 1995. The day began like any other, but it became a nightmare that horrified the nation.

AN ARMY OF ANGELS

The front of the Alfred P. Murrah Building looked as if it had been scooped out by a giant shovel. Floors stood exposed like cliffs on a mountainside. Nearby buildings

＊ ＊ ＊ ★

were also damaged by the force of the blast. Fire poured out of parked cars. Wounded and dazed men and women began to fill the streets. Scores of people buried under the rubble were suffocating from smoke and dust. Still others were stranded on top floors.

At once, a heroic effort to treat the injured and to help trapped victims began. The rescuers included police, coworkers, firefighters, and passersby. Black, white, and Hispanic people—the wealthy as well as the homeless—all pitched in. One visitor said it was as if "an army of angels" came to the aid of Oklahoma City in its time of need.

Rescue workers try to find people who might be buried under the rubble.

* * * *

One such angel was Rebecca Anderson, a thirty-seven-year-old nurse. While smoke **billowed** out of the shell of the building, she rushed inside to help. Her husband later said he was not surprised by her actions. Rebecca was the type who took in stray dogs and was always kind to

Oklahoma City firefighters take a break between shifts at the main emergency staging area north of the Murrah Federal Building.

* * * *

Firefighters and a rescue dog

HEROIC HOUNDS

Urban Search and Rescue (USAR) teams brought in sniffer dogs. These animals are specially trained to find men and women trapped under wreckage caused by an event such as an explosion or an earthquake. With their keen sense of smell, the rescue dogs can detect people even when they are buried deep under concrete and plaster.

strangers. While working in the crumbling building, she was struck on the head by falling concrete. Rebecca Anderson died four days later.

About one hundred rescue workers suffered some sort of injury. Giant slabs of concrete dangled from upper floors and fell without warning. Knifelike pieces of glass and jagged metal poked out of the wreckage. Yet the army of angels worked. Mostly they dug, brick by brick, with their bare hands, trying to free buried men and women.

Police sergeant Kevin G. Thompson was one of those who ventured into the collapsing shell of the building. Thompson's story reflects the dangers and frustrations faced by the rescue workers:

A fire captain almost up against the north wall said he had found another victim alive, a woman. He pointed to

13

This view of the Murrah building shows how the bomb ripped off its front and exposed its floors.

a large pile of concrete. I could now hear this lady talking to us. She was very calm and did not sound as if she was in pain. I bent down and looked but could only see a small part of her lower back. I looked at what was on

top of her—tons and tons of concrete covered almost all of her. I felt absolutely useless, and I knew the fire captain felt the same. It was in his eyes and face. We had only our hands, no tools to work with . . . I noticed debris falling; as I looked up, I could see that about 10 feet [3 meters] above us was a 10-by-20 foot [3 m-by-6 m] slab of concrete hanging by only a couple pieces of rebar [a steel rod used in rein-forced concrete]. I knew that if it fell, we would die.

The trapped woman whom Sergeant Thompson aided was Daina Bradley. That morning she had gone to the Murrah Building on a simple mission: to apply for a Social Security card. She brought her mother and two young children with her to the Social Security office. In order to free Bradley from the wreckage, a doctor had to amputate her right leg. The amputation was done on the spot, without the aid of painkilling medication. Daina Bradley

Aren Almon-Kok holds her infant daughter, Baylee Almon, who was killed in the bombing.

recovered, but her mother and two children were killed in the blast. A year later she remained bitter about the bombing, but Bradley believed her loved ones had found peace in heaven. She said, "I think about them . . . smiling and doing fine. No pain. No worries."

What most concerned the rescuers was the fate of the children in the building. The second-floor day-care center—America's Kids—was in the hardest hit section of the building. A college student named Heather Taylor reported: "The firemen were bringing out so many dead [children]. As soon as I would take one child, another child was laid next to it. I remember one man, a bystander who was helping me, said, 'Why all of the children, why?' I just watched him cry."

Frantic relatives asked survivors for news about their wives, husbands, aunts, and uncles. Grimmest of all were the parents desperately searching for their children. A witness named Jerry Griffin said, "I saw an elderly white woman carrying a black baby. A young black woman ran toward her screaming, 'My baby! Is that my baby?' When she got within 5 feet [1.5 m] of the child and saw its face, she turned and continued running, screaming, 'Where's my baby? Where's my baby?'"

About ninety minutes after the blast the rescuers were ordered off the site. A rumor, which proved to be untrue, said a second bomb had been planted at the building and would soon go off. At first, some rescuers refused to leave

A firefighter with a sniffer dog.

DEPRESSED DOGS

Handlers of the rescue dogs claimed that once a dog discovered

a body, he or she became noticeably sad and often whined.

the victims they were aiding, but eventually everyone obeyed police orders to clear the area. The rescue crews returned after forty-five minutes. Precious time had been lost by the false bomb report. In the evening a dismal rain fell, further hampering rescue efforts.

By midnight the last living person was taken from the rubble. Rescuers worked through the night and over the next several days, but crews found nothing other than bodies. The federal building, once a collection of busy offices, had become a mass grave.

THE SUSPECT

An hour and twenty minutes after the bombing, Oklahoma Highway Patrol Officer Charles Hanger was driving along Highway I-35, about 75 miles (121 km) from the blast area. His squad car radio buzzed with news of the crime at the federal building. The officer saw a beat-up 1977 Mercury.

McVeigh's car, parked ahead of the police cars, was stopped on the highway because it had no license plates.

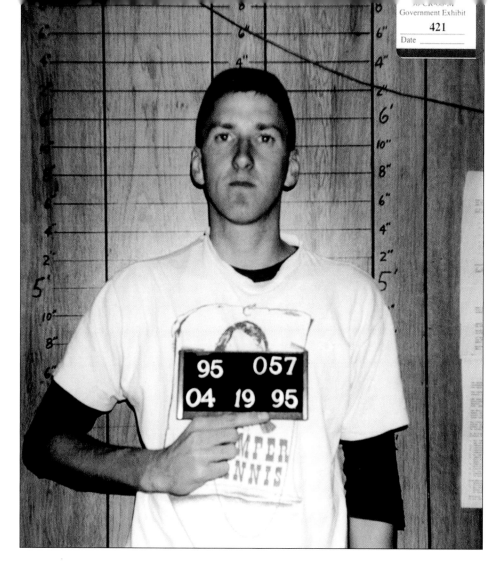

Timothy McVeigh, pictured here as jail inmate number 95-057, was initially held on traffic and weapons charges.

He stopped the vehicle because it had no license plates. The driver was twenty-seven-year-old Timothy McVeigh.

Hanger asked why the car was without plates. McVeigh explained he had recently purchased the car, and the plates were still in the mail. Did he have a bill of sale for the Mercury? Yes, but not on him. Hanger noticed a bulge under McVeigh's jacket. What was it? McVeigh admitted it was a pistol. Hanger arrested McVeigh and took him to jail. McVeigh went peacefully, offering no resistance.

THE ONGOING CONFLICT

A truck bomb exploded below New York's 110-story World Trade Center on February 26, 1993, killing six people and injuring more than one thousand others. Four Muslim men were convicted of the crime. (A Muslim is a follower of the religion of Islam.) Many Muslims, especially in the Arab world, are angered by U.S. support of Israel, the Jewish state in the Middle East created in the late 1940s in the region formerly known as Palestine.

The twin towers of New York's World Trade center building were damaged after the February 1993 attack. Both towers were destroyed on September 11, 2001, when two hijacked passenger airliners slammed into them.

Meanwhile rumors that the bomb was planted by Arab **fanatics** swept the nation. Acting on the rumors, police stopped and questioned people simply because they looked as if they came from the Middle East.

The date of the bombing—April 19—intrigued members of the Federal Bureau of Investigation (FBI). On April 19, 1993, eighty members of a religious **cult** called the Branch Davidians were killed at Waco, Texas, during a confrontation with federal law enforcement officers. The Branch Davidians perished in a fire that authorities claimed was set by the cult members themselves. The Davidians, however, believed the fire was the result of an attack by federal agents on their compound. Now, exactly two years later, some FBI agents wondered if the Oklahoma City bombing was an act of revenge committed by persons who hated the federal government.

In the town of Perry, Oklahoma, Timothy McVeigh was about to face a judge. He was jail inmate number 95-057, charged with traffic and gun violations. Unknown to

David Koresh, leader of the Branch Davidians.

Eighty members of the Branch Davidian religious cult were killed in Waco, Texas, during this fire on April 19, 1993.

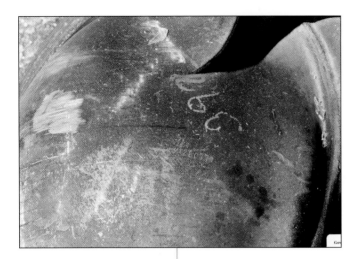

FBI agents found this serial number on the rear axle of the Ryder truck and traced the truck to Timothy McVeigh.

McVeigh, the FBI was building a case against him as the bomber in the Oklahoma City attack. Some 600 feet (183 m) from the blast site investigators discovered the mangled rear axle of a rental truck. The serial number on the axle was traced to the Ryder Company and eventually to Timothy McVeigh. The FBI filed charges against McVeigh, and he was kept in jail. Had the FBI not intervened, it was likely the judge would have released inmate number 95-057 on bail.

Newspapers and TV commentators announced that the government had a prime suspect. Wearing a bright orange jumpsuit, McVeigh was led out of jail and taken to more

McVeigh being led out of jail surrounded by guards; he was at that moment the most hated man in America.

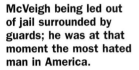

* * * *

McVeigh was transferred to more secure jail facilities at nearby Tinker Air Force Base, shown here.

secure facilities at Tinker Air Force Base. Crowds shouted, "Baby killer!" "Murderer!" Overnight, Timothy McVeigh had become the most hated man in America.

HONORING THE VICTIMS

In the weeks and months that followed, Oklahoma City counted its losses. In all, 168 people had died; 164 inside the Murrah Building, 3 in nearby structures, and 1 who had been walking on the sidewalk. Nineteen of the dead were children. Some 850 people suffered injuries. More than three hundred downtown buildings reported some degree of damage. The value of property lost was placed at $652 million.

The devastation felt by the people of Oklahoma City could not be measured. Almost half the population of Oklahoma City attended funerals in the weeks following the bombing. A study revealed other bleak consequences: 30 Oklahoma City children were orphaned; 219 children lost at least one

★ ★ ★ ★

Debris from the blast caused damage to buildings and parked cars blocks away from the Murrah building.

Memorial service for Linda McKinney, an office manager killed inside the building; the service was held May 3, 1995.

The Oklahoma City National Memorial seen from a distance

parent; 462 people became homeless; 7,000 men and women lost jobs because their workplace was either destroyed or damaged.

Yet the tragedy did not destroy the city's spirit. Instead of allowing grief to consume them, the people concentrated on turning the wreckage of the federal building into a **shrine.** Residents hoped to fashion a monument that would forever honor the dead, the injured, and those who worked so bravely to save lives. The monument project began the healing process, which the city badly needed.

Workers cleared away the ruins of the old federal building and plans were made to build a **memorial** on its grounds. A memorial is an object—a remembrance—that tells the story of a person or an event to future generations. A gravestone, a statue, or a tree can serve as a memorial.

A LOOK AT OKLAHOMA CITY

With a population of almost 450,000, Oklahoma City is both the capital of Oklahoma and its largest city. The city was born on April 22, 1889, when the federal government opened the Oklahoma Territory to settlers on a first-come, first-claim basis. By nightfall on the first day of the "land rush," the previously unpopulated site of the future state capital held a tent camp settlement of ten thousand people.

Since the Oklahoma City bombing was a national tragedy, it was determined that its remembrance should be preserved as a national memorial.

As of the year 2002, the United States had 28 national memorials. These are memorials recognized by the government as having special meaning to all Americans. The government can add more national memorials to its list at any time. Some of the more famous national memorials include the Lincoln Memorial and the Vietnam Veterans Memorial (The Wall) in Washington, D.C., and the USS *Arizona* Memorial in Hawaii.

Map of Oklahoma. Oklahoma City is in the center of the state.

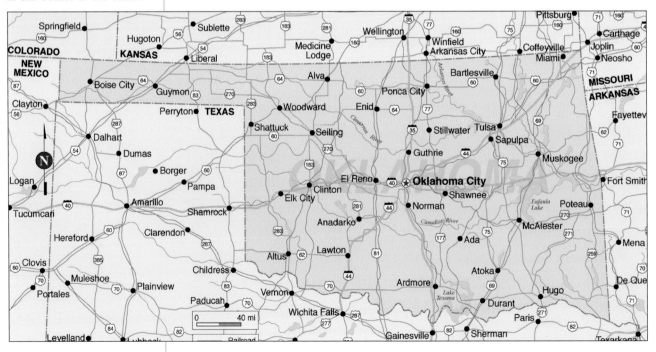

* * * *

The Lincoln Memorial in Washington, D.C., receives millions of visitors each year.

Oklahoma City Mayor Ron Norick appointed a 350-member committee to determine what sort of structure

Oklahoma City Mayor Ron Norick started the memorial project by appointing a 350-member committee made up primarily of survivors and relatives of the dead.

should be built on the site of the Murrah Building. The committee was made up largely of survivors, members of the various rescue crews, and relatives of the dead. In the fall of 1996 the committee became the Oklahoma City National Memorial Foundation. The foundation asked artists and architects to submit designs. In a matter of months, more than six hundred suggestions were received at the foundation's office.

27

THE MEMORIAL MISSION STATEMENT

Adopted March 26, 1996, the Memorial Mission Statement suggested themes and goals for artists who hoped to design the Oklahoma City National Memorial. The statement was written by a committee that represented survivors, rescue workers, and families of victims. Here are two suggestions advanced by the statement:

Peace—The Memorial Complex should provide a quiet, peaceful setting where visitors have an opportunity for reflection. Many participants suggest using natural elements such as trees, flowers, gardens, or water to create a serene atmosphere.

Spirituality and Hope—The memorial should be powerful, awe-inspiring, and convey the deep sense of loss caused by the bombing. By the same token, it should evoke feelings of compassion and hope, and inspire visitors to live their lives meaningfully. It should speak of the community and nation that was so evident in the wake of the attack.

How does one memorialize such a terrible event? Some of the suggestions were novel. One artist wanted to focus on the victims who were children by building a friendly looking giant teddy bear at the site. Most proposals included 168 objects to remind viewers of the dead. An interesting plan proposed a field of 168 bronze bells. A design that was chosen as one of the finalists in the competition featured a circular garden surrounded by a wall of 168 trees.

During rescue operations people stuffed gifts into the chain-link fence that surrounded the bomb site. The fence became part of the memorial and people
leave gifts there to this day.

The memorial's Reflecting Pool, which is less than one inch deep, represents the healing power of water.

Days after the bombing, Oklahoma City dwellers made their own choice of a remembrance. People began placing little gifts on a hastily erected chain-link fence that was put up around the bombing site. The gifts, which included notes and handwritten poems, were designed to cheer up the rescue crews. Children were the biggest gift-givers, often donating stuffed animals or baseball caps. That simple chain-link fence was later made a permanent fixture of the memorial. Today it is called the Memorial Fence, and visitors continue to slip items into its wire diamonds.

On June 24, 1997, the foundation selected a design created by the husband-and-wife team of Hans and Torrey Butzer. Both artists were graduates of the University of Texas at Austin. Torrey Butzer was born in the town of

The Field of Empty Chairs represents those who died in the bombing.

Nowata, Oklahoma. Work on the Butzer creation began, and early in the year 2000 the outdoor portion of the memorial was complete.

Towering above the site stand the Gates of Time, which mark two entrances to the memorial. The East Gate bears the time 9:01, while the West Gate reads 9:03. Thus the time 9:02 A.M.—the moment of the bombing—is framed at the Reflecting Pool between the two gates. Victims are honored in the Field of Empty Chairs, an arrangement of 168 bronze and stone chairs that represent each life lost. Hans Butzer explained: "Like an empty chair at the dinner table, we are always aware of the presence of a loved one's absence." The chairs are placed in nine rows to stand for the nine floors of the federal building. Nineteen of the chairs are smaller because they represent the children who died. At night the chairs are lit by individual lights, which shine as **beacons** proclaiming life after death.

Across from the Reflecting Pool rises the Survivor Tree. The tree, an American elm, dates back to the 1920s. It once stood in the parking lot across from the Murrah Building. The elm lived through the bombing, even though cars around it burst into flame and blew up. The Survivor Tree reminds us that family and community life continue despite the loss of loved ones. Nearby is the Rescuers' Orchard, which is represented by rows of fruit trees. The design team said, "[We] began to imagine an army of helpers, rushing in from all directions . . . We have translated this army of helpers into an army of fruit trees, marching forth from the street's edge to surround the Survivor Tree."

The Survivor Tree, an eighty-year-old American elm that survived the blast, reminds visitors that family life continues despite the loss of loved ones.

President Clinton dedicated the Oklahoma City National Memorial on April 19, 2000, exactly five years after the bombing.

Most national memorials are paid for by the American taxpayer, but the Oklahoma City National Memorial Foundation was determined to raise most of its own funds. The project cost about $30 million. The foundation asked for donations, and the money was raised. Donations came in the form of large checks given by corporations and bags of pennies contributed by schoolchildren. Funds also came from the state of Oklahoma and the U.S. government.

The Oklahoma City National Memorial was officially dedicated on April 19, 2000, exactly five years after the truck bomb shattered so many lives. The principal speaker at the dedication was President Bill Clinton. The President focused on the victims: "Five years ago the cowards who killed them made a choice—a choice to attack this building and the people in it, because they wanted to strike a blow at America's **heartland,** at the core of our nation's being. This was an attack on all America and every American. Five years later, we are here

Michael Fortier, pictured left, who knew of McVeigh's plan to bomb the Murrah building, but failed to tell the police.

CONSPIRACY THEORY

A third man, Michael Fortier, pleaded guilty to having prior knowledge of the bomb plot but failing to alert police. Fortier received a twelve-year prison sentence. Many Americans believe there were other conspirators, or helpers, in this crime. However, the FBI claimed everyone involved was brought to justice.

because you made a choice, a choice to choose hope and love over despair and hatred."

FINAL JUSTICE

After a series of trials Timothy McVeigh and an **accomplice,** Terry L. Nichols, were convicted of the bombing. Nichols was sentenced to life in prison without possibility of parole. At the time of the attack Nichols was in his farmhouse in Kansas, but he was convicted of helping McVeigh assemble the bomb. McVeigh, the lone bomber and mastermind of the scheme, received the death penalty.

Terry Nichols, McVeigh's accomplice in the Oklahoma City bombing

Timothy McVeigh grew up in a small town in northwest New York state. While he was in high school his parents

35

⋆ ⋆ ⋆ ⋆

divorced, and friends claimed he became **sullen.** McVeigh joined the army and served in the Persian Gulf War, which was fought in 1990 and 1991. An excellent soldier, he was awarded a **Bronze Star** for bravery. After leaving the army,

THE WAR ON TERRORISM

On September 11, 2001, Arab terrorists hijacked four passenger-jet airliners. The hijackers intentionally crashed one plane into the Pentagon in Arlington, Virginia. Another plane plunged to the ground in rural Pennsylvania, and the other two were flown into the World Trade Center towers in New York City. About three thousand people died in the attacks. The September 11 attacks stand as the nation's worst terrorist incident. After the attacks, President George W. Bush proclaimed the United States would wage a war on terrorism.

The World Trade Center's twin towers shortly before their collapse.

McVeigh drifted from job to job. He was also drawn to political groups that opposed the federal government. McVeigh believed the 1993 deaths of the Branch Davidians at Waco, Texas, were the result of a deliberate act of murder committed by government agents.

McVeigh in his army days

Under the law, placing a bomb near a crowded building is a terrorist act. A terrorist is an individual who is willing to use terror in order to dramatize a political or religious cause. The 1995 bombing was, at the time, the deadliest act of terrorism ever committed in the United States.

On June 11, 2001, Timothy McVeigh was put to death by lethal injection at the federal penitentiary in Terre Haute, Indiana. In open court he never confessed to his crime, but in interviews with writers he admitted responsibility for the bombing. He claimed the federal government was his enemy and that, therefore, the federal building in Oklahoma City was a "legitimate target." McVeigh called the death of nineteen children collateral damage. The term "collateral damage" was often used in the Gulf War to describe bomb damage inflicted on structures and people other than the bomb's primary target.

McVeigh saw himself as a **martyr** in a crusade against the government. The term "martyr" is usually applied to a religious person who chooses to suffer death in order to uphold his or her convictions. FBI agent Danny Defenbaugh, the leading investigator in the bombing case, said, "[McVeigh's] not a martyr. He's a cold-blooded killer." Most Americans agreed with Defenbaugh.

★ ★ ★ ★

A National Park Service Ranger poses at the memorial.

WE COME HERE TO REMEMBER
THOSE WHO WERE KILLED, THOSE WHO SURVIVED AND THOSE CHANGED FOREVER.
MAY ALL WHO LEAVE HERE KNOW THE IMPACT OF VIOLENCE.
MAY THIS MEMORIAL OFFER COMFORT, STRENGTH, PEACE, HOPE AND SERENITY.

SOLEMN DUTY

All national memorials are run by the National Park Service. The uniformed guides are park service employees and are properly called rangers.

"WE COME HERE TO REMEMBER . . ."

Begin a visit to the Oklahoma City National Memorial by entering the outdoor plaza at either of the two Gates of Time. The entire outdoor exhibit is called the Symbolic Memorial.

This is an appropriate name because symbols are used everywhere on the plaza. The Reflecting Pool, which is only three quarters of an inch (1.9 centimeters) deep, represents the soothing power of water to heal wounds. The pool also stands for those people who were changed forever by the bombing. The 168 empty chairs symbolize the lives lost. Each chair bears the name of a victim. A guard rail bars casual visitors from approaching the chairs. Close relatives and friends of the dead are permitted to leave flowers and other gifts.

Uniformed guides work in the plaza, assisting visitors and answering questions. The guides are on duty during daylight hours. The plaza never closes. Many people enjoy strolling around the Reflecting Pool at night.

Beyond the Rescuers' Orchard stands the Memorial Center, an interactive museum and learning facility. The museum occupies 30,000 square feet (2,787 square meters) in what was once the newspaper offices of the *Journal Record*. The building, constructed in 1923, suffered heavy damage during the blast. Several of the building's broken walls are preserved to allow visitors to grasp the force of the explosion.

The Memorial Center is devoted largely to the dead and injured victims of the attack. Little **mementos** of the dead—a watch, a pair of eyeglasses, and a child's toy—are on display. The story of the bombing is presented in chapters entitled "Chaos and Confusion," "Survivor Experiences," "Rescue and Recovery," "Watching and Waiting," "Remembrance and Rebuilding," and—finally—"Hope."

Visitors follow these chapters through powerful photographs, video clips, and oral histories told by the people who were there.

Perhaps the most stunning of all the Memorial Center exhibits is "A Hearing." To view this exhibit, guests sit facing what appears to be a blank wall. Taped words are heard of officers conducting a routine hearing regarding water resources. Suddenly an explosion—the actual tape-recorded sound of the blast—interrupts the meeting. The room goes dark. The once blank wall bursts into light and shows individual photos of all 168 people who died. Many visitors leave "A Hearing" with tears streaming down their faces.

A visit to the Oklahoma City National Memorial is a solemn yet uplifting experience. The memorial asks a question of its visitors: Can hope rise from tragedy? The memorial answers that question with a resounding YES!

FAST FACTS ABOUT THE MEMORIAL

- **Location**—Between NW Fourth and Sixth Streets and Robinson and Harvey Avenues in downtown Oklahoma City.

- **Addresses**—Street address: 620 N. Harvey Avenue; mailing address: PO Box 323, Oklahoma City, OK 73101

- **Dedicated**—April 19, 2000.

- **Cost of Construction**—About $30 million, most of which was raised by private donations.

- **Layout**—The site is divided into two parts: the Outdoor Symbolic Memorial and the Memorial Center Museum.

The outdoor plaza covers 3.3 acres (1.3 hectares), while the museum contains exhibits on two floors.

- **Hours and Fees**—The Outdoor Symbolic Memorial is open 24 hours a day, 7 days a week, and there is no charge to enter. The Museum is open 9 A.M. to 6 P.M. Monday through Saturday, and 1 A.M. through 6 P.M. Sundays. The museum charges admission based on age. Group rates are available.

- **The Oklahoma City National Memorial Institute for the Prevention of Terrorism (MIPT)**—The MIPT is a vital element of the Oklahoma City National Memorial. The MIPT sponsors conferences and research into terrorism. Offices of the MIPT are housed within the museum building, but few of its functions are open to the public.

Glossary

accomplice—helper or a partner in an action

beacons—shining lights

billowed—poured out in thick clouds like smoke from a fire

Bronze Star—a medal given to American service men and women for bravery during military operations

cult—a small group of religious extremists who worship a person, a principle, or a god

dazed—stunned, shocked, or rendered helpless by a terrible event

fanatic—a person who is especially zealous about a particular cause

frantic—desperate with fear or anxiety

heartland—the central region of a country

martyr—a person who suffers death rather than violate a principle

mementos—objects, usually small, that remind a viewer of a person or an event

memorial—an object that tells the story of a person or an event to future generations

resounded—filled with sound

shards—small, knifelike pieces of glass or metal

shrine—a tomb or a container that holds sacred relics

sullen—sad or depressed

symbol—a representation, one thing representing another thing

Timeline: The Oklahoma

The Alfred P. Murrah Building in downtown Oklahoma City is completed; when fully staffed, it will serve as a workplace for about five hundred people.

APRIL 19
At 9:02 A.M. a truck bomb explodes in front of the Murrah Building killing 168 people and injuring hundreds more. An hour and twenty minutes later a policeman arrests Timothy McVeigh for a traffic violation on a highway outside of Oklahoma City.

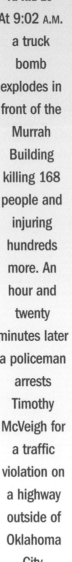

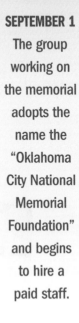

APRIL 23
President Bill Clinton proclaims a national day of mourning and orders all American flags to be flown at half-staff.

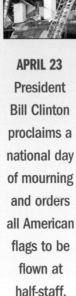

JUNE 10
Oklahoma City attorney Robert Johnson heads a committee decide on a suitable memorial for the tragedy.

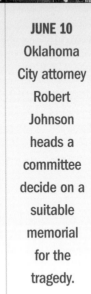

SEPTEMBER 1
The group working on the memorial adopts the name the "Oklahoma City National Memorial Foundation" and begins to hire a paid staff.

JUNE 24
The selection committee of the Oklahoma City National Memorial Foundation chooses a design submitted by the husband-and-wife team of Hans and Torrey Butzer.

City National Memorial

1998 | 2000 | 2001

OCTOBER 25
Ground is broken to build the memorial on the site of the Murrah Building.

APRIL 19
Exactly five years after the bombing, the Oklahoma City National Memorial is dedicated; President Bill Clinton is the principal speaker.

FEBRUARY 19
The Oklahoma City National Memorial Center, an interactive museum, is opened across from the outdoor plaza. President George W. Bush takes part in the dedication ceremony.

JUNE 11
Timothy McVeigh is executed for planting the Oklahoma City bomb.

45

To Find Out More

BOOKS

Cole, Michael D. *The Siege at Waco: Deadly Inferno.* Berkeley Heights, NJ: Enslow Publishers, 1999.

Fridell, Ron. *Terrorism: Political Violence at Home and Abroad.* Berkeley Heights, NJ: Enslow Publishers, 2001.

Reedy, Jerry. *Oklahoma—America the Beautiful, Second Series.* Danbury, CT: Childrens Press, 1998.

Sherrow, Victoria. *The Oklahoma City Bombing: Terror in the Heartland.* Berkeley Heights, NJ: Enslow Publishers, 1998.

Sonder, Ben. *The Militia Movement: Fighters of the Far Right.* Danbury, CT: Franklin Watts, 2000.

ONLINE SITES

Oklahoma City National Memorial Home Page
www.nps.gov/okci/

Oklahoma City National Memorial Institute for the Prevention of Terrorism (MIPT)
www.mipt.org/

Oklahoma City Visitors Center—Tourism and Conventions
www.okccub.org/

Index

Bold numbers indicate illustrations.

About the Author

R. Conrad Stein was born and raised in Chicago. At age eighteen he joined the United States Marines and served three years. He later attended the University of Illinois, where he received a degree in history. Mr. Stein is a full-time author of books for young readers, and over the years he has published more than one hundred titles. He lives in Chicago with his wife (children's book author Deborah Kent) and their daughter, Janna.

Late in the year 2001, Mr. Stein made a special trip to Oklahoma City to see the Oklahoma City National Memorial. He spoke with members of the staff and with rangers who serve as guides. The author wishes to thank all those he interviewed for their help and their courtesy. Joining hundreds of tourists, Mr. Stein visited the Memorial Center Museum and walked about the Outdoor Symbolic Memorial. He found the experience to be uplifting, even spiritual.